I WILL COME WITH A LIGHTHOUSE

I WILL COME WITH A LIGHTHOUSE

SAYAN AICH BHOWMIK

Hawakal
PUBLISHERS

New Delhi | Calcutta

HAWAKAL
New Delhi | Calcutta

HAWAKAL PUBLISHERS PRIVATE LIMITED
70 B/9 Amritpuri, East of Kailash, New Delhi
65 33/1/2 K B Sarani, Mall Road, Calcutta 80

Email info@hawakal.com
Website www.hawakal.com

Cover designed by Bitan Chakraborty

First edition (paperback) January 2022

ISBN: 978-93-91431-44-0 (paperback)

Price: INR 250 | USD 12.99

for

Raangta, my daughter

CONTENTS

ACKNOWLEDGEMENTS

I will Come with a Lighthouse has been almost 4 years in the making. These poems are a result of a negotiation with notions of identity and the spectre of belonging, a constant grappling with versions of the self and their idiosyncrasies and an angst that has characterised my being over the last half a decade. They can be also read as meditations on love, longing, loss and a yearning for times and places that we only call our own, either in memories and dreams. I take this opportunity to thank the editors who had overseen the publication of some of the poems in their respective journals. Kiriti Sengupta of Hawakal Publishers was the driving force behind this venture coming to fruition. His sharp insights and inputs were invaluable and I hope this book does justice to the trust and faith he decided to put in a debut collection. My heartfelt gratitude to Bitan Chakraborty for coming up with a visually stunning cover.

The premise for my fondness for literature had been laid in school, by the likes of Mr. Surath Roy, Mrs. Manjula Banerjee and Mr. Christopher Foran. I hope I can be half as magical and inspiring to my students in my classroom as you were for me.

Suchismita Raha, formerly of St. Thomas Girls'

School and now associated with Vivekananda Mission School, Kolkata, has been a mentor to me for as long as I can remember. I try very hard, each day, to repay the love and kindness she had bestowed upon me, since I was 16.

Dr. Abin Chakraborty has been my go-to person for the last decade and a half. His astute observations and criticism has led to a sharpening of my poetic sensibilities. My friends who make *Plato's Caves Online* the success that it is today, I thank with a lion's share of my heart.

My parents I could never thank enough. But this is a good place to start. My grandmother whom I miss dearly and whose presence I hope the readers will be able to feel in many of the poems. And finally, my wife, Satabdi, who has known me for almost half my age and deserves all the credit in the world for putting up with a dreamer.

Some of the poems in this collection have previously seen the light of day in the following journals and magazines: *Miraas, The Asian Signature Journal, Sonic Boom, Poetica Review, Yawp, The Kindle Magazine Online, Kashmir Lit-Resistance Issue, Mountain Ink, Saaranga, The Metaworker, Chaos: Local Gems Press, Joao Roque Journal, The Pangolin Review, The Brasilia Review, The Harbinger Asylum, Setu Bilingual Journal, Prachya Review, Eunoia Review, Delmarva Review* and *The Punch Magazine*.

The Moths

Calcutta returns home,
Inside me.
I count the cars
With their seat-belts around my tongue.
My eye-lashes sweep the streets
A storm from another time
And whatever remains of the day
Stays back like crematorium ash
The dead having already escaped.
All the available pin-codes
Sit with missing story-tellers
And listens to ships returning
To empty harbours.
My Janus city has two names
Both quiet like people
Who have already removed themselves
From telephone directories.
At night,
Moths travel between Calcutta and Kolkata
Planning a trip to the moon.

Longing and Solitude

When We Meet

In this town
strangers come
leaving a bit of themselves
pinned on the mists
the hills wear
as Kashmiri pashmina.
Some stay back
ploughing the air,
with long distance phone calls
to people, whose names
have disappeared
from telephone directories.
At day's end, when the lights come on
and the rains cry
over unclaimed letters at the post office,
these men
sit with highways on their table
throwing stars as dice
staking their childhood.
They walk out on milky ways
spread outside their doors.
Far away, the telephone wires
sizzle in the dark
With the news of our meeting.

Certainties

Tonight, almost every bit of me
has been compelled to write about certainties.
I'm certain, the last train has left
for the small towns which don't find
a place to rest on maps.
By the time
your mind has stopped oscillating
between two thoughts
and finds one of those
park benches between them
a really drunk night
would have walked onto the stage
with dead stars
on its lapel.
By this time
no song remains trapped
between two radio stations.
And finally, a random passer-by
has stopped at the community tap
to drink the rains
whose arrival, the weathermen
got wrong last week.

After Dinner

After dinner
the entire city
speaks through my radio,
each voice like leftover food
sitting on my table.
The cutlery I bring out
to feast on this
directory of longing.
Later, I wipe off the moon
with the napkin
of empty streets.
And the irritating sound
of the sky dragging its feet.

Men From Salamanca

During warm summer nights
when horses ran to their imaginary homes
across Andalusia
and a sad light kept dripping
from the stars
men from Salamanca
would play on their violins
songs about miners
about mirrors that failed
to show what we wanted to see
about train whistles heard at the dead of night
about nights that refuse to end
about dawns that refuse to begin.
The men have left with their shadows
only that sad light from the stars
keeps dripping.

Letting Go

Of all the times, I've let go
of people, only once
the cigarette in my hand
wasn't the only thing that was burning.
I came home
and set a river to my heart.

Chessboard

Death no longer comes to my door,
with the sombre knocking.
His footsteps walk into my room
like an unexpected guest.
And I always have the chessboard ready
if he wins, I lose–
if I win, I lose.

The Last Time

It was the day, when he
who loved his afternoon nap
was seen for one final time.
The post-box outside his door
had been emptied of the brown leaves
that had been living there since autumn.
The electricity bills had been paid
and a prediction for evening rain
lay outside his door.
He was seen sitting
by the window scribbling furiously.
If it hadn't been for the suicide note
that filled the entire neighbourhood
with the scent of *attar*
no one would have known
that it was the last day
when he who loved his afternoon nap
was seen for the last time.

My Twin

I have never found
it in my heart to clean my room.
I like it muddy and untidy
the kind of chaos that accompanies
a frantic search for the passport
at the airport.
A madness walking naked
turning my walls into exit routes
where trains travel between cities
setting fire to the night.
In a jar, I keep a sad river,
which my mother brought from Varanasi
and in a bowl the hunger of a crematorium.
From the book-shelves
Shahid mourns for Kashmir
Bukowski is furious at a type writer
and Cohen is putting oceans to sleep.
These men whisper
when the stars come out.
At times I see someone like me
made of paper and glass
lying on the sofa.
In the glass I see myself
with the paper he slits my throat.

A Room Too Small For Sunsets

The toaster has thrown up
the alarm has been snoozed twice
and the coffee beans– hard as immigration rules
lie scattered, before they walk towards
their expiry dates.
In this room which is
too small for sunsets
I sit by a window
and watch the city
not on anybody's map
become a river.
The streets that play
hide and seek with the traffic lights
will come wandering inside my head.
At night, I will
sleep with my fingers
On the zippers of the sky.

The Stamp Collector

The stamp collector
sits at the entrance of the night
sorting post cards from towns
he'd visited in his dreams.
There are shabby taverns
Inside which labourers with soiled hands
and darker tomorrows sit and hope
that time will pass them by
without a cursory glance.
Someone in another town
goes undressing the skies
and unlocking old stories
buzzing around eager children.
Sitting under an autumn
our stamp collector lets brown leaves
grow on him.
It is the kind of solitude which even
a bartender is afraid to cure.

The Other Side

I'm so deep inside the night
that even if I decide to walk on
I might not get to the other side.
The road goes through a keyhole
sits on sharp pencil tips
waiting for the right words.
I sit with the solitude
of an astronaut trapped in space.
The night is so deep
it has no other side.

Of Simple Things

I woke up earlier than usual
to write on the remains of the night.
I told myself
that it must be a simple poem
it should be a simple act
like opening the fridge
and a simple disappointment
of finding it empty.
No prospect of negotiations with former lovers
who spoke to me like Public Address Systems
when all I wanted to do
was stand like a streetlight
in the rains.
It should be a simple straightforward act
Like tying the noose around your neck
And kicking the chair.

Lighting a Cigarette

Sometimes, I steal matchsticks
from the kitchen drawer
turn on the gas
and see Jupiter turning slowly
in the blue flame.
To set fire to an entire planet
still remains a favourite fantasy.
I keep playing the image
over and over in my head
rotating slender bushfires
between my fingers.
All the while
hoping that someone would
take a photograph of me
my back towards the camera
lighting a cigarette with the sun.

Time

On afternoons like these
the calendars hanging on our walls
melt like wax
the weeks and months in black ink
smudging into a single pickle.
The May breeze walks in
through the curtains
heavier than oceans
settling on the strings of your sitar.
Your fingers bleed
cut by strips of lightning
as you play a *raaga*
to put me to sleep.
Instead, I sit in a corner
sewing patterns of rain
onto a pullover of longing.

On Love

First Time

Across that long courtyard
where I once sat
eating pistachios and drinking tea
your ghost talks with mine
in a tongue
which turns words into air
the kind which remains
between lips
meeting for the first time.

Folded Sky

I fold the corners
of a very desperate sky.
The stars I throw away,
on highways that know
where they are heading.
I chisel my name
on the sadness of the sky's dark blue.
The space between the clouds
I tie with guitar strings
which catch fire every time
someone utters your name.
My neatly folded sky
has cigarette burns all over its skin.

Somewhere Else

I don't need to be drunk to want you
and you need not be sober to refuse.
You could just move your fingers
around the rim of the glass...
again and again.
I'd still be at the table
plucking the stars from inside your clothes
working on the order of words
I've been meaning to speak.
After all said and done
isn't death another way
of being accepted somewhere else?

Elsewhere

I remember last winter
I ran into someone at the marketplace
where lonely men display their solitude in crystal jars
someone wearing the same perfume
that you smeared on yourself after a shower.
The highways that have howled at midnight
sat between us waiting for winter to melt.
You have uprooted every milestone
and brought down every lighthouse
that could have led me to you.
I have realised that
even though the highway and the winter
might return
they will now take me somewhere else.

Of Previous Births

Is it possible then
that the moment you undress
the tungsten bulb melts
on your moonlight skin.
A country in exile
dreams in the language of return
where everyone looks
like everyone else.
Outside the night moves on tiptoe
and our ceiling opens up
to the counting of the stars
when morning arrives
like the rightful heir
my fingers are laced with *attar*
orbitting the planets on your breasts.
Your clothes catch fire
and in that glow
I see your lips move
and write in air
my names from previous births.

The Last Pages

This dawn has been
the softest part of the night.
The morning further softens
when you press the sky
between your lips.
Not one star untouched
not one star un-tasted.
I've dipped my tongue
in the black of your hair
and squeeze myself through
the space between two thoughts.
I arrive at the news stands
with cigarette in hand, to find
they have written about us
in the last pages of the night.

Of Things Like The Sky

I've emptied so much
of my everydays
into my apartment
that now, even I smell of
burnt toast and washing powder.
The sun inside the fridge
rises when the door is open
and I squeeze myself inside
a long distance phone call
to walk between unknown voices.
The days are clerks going to office
same routes, same trajectories
without fail, without orgasm.
My room, which had once slept
with arms wide open
giving refuge to women,
is now a Jesus of 18X12,
nails all over the walls,
from which hangs
nights of yesterdays.
I sit with unpaid bills
waiting for the things, like the sky
and your heart
to crack open.

Nine Lives or So

Every Friday at the local market
I'd see her buying clay pots
to plant her poems
a Jerry can to water them
just in case it didn't rain
for a couple of days
and small packets of manure
for words that failed
to howl at the moon.
I sat on a bench
and watched her go from shop to shop
her white apron
an invisible shield
against the dirt of the world.
Later, the children gathered around her
and she patiently handed over
to each of them
unruly rivers flowing
from within the folds of her dress
instructing them on how
to make paper boats
when the rains arrived.
When evening came
and the pub opened its doors

we would wait till the air was so heavy
with grief that we could
write our names on it.
Later, I often saw her
running her long fingers
over a tropical storm
like one tends a cat with the intention
Of inheriting all its nine lives.

711 Windows

The last time I counted
711 windows inside your clothes
the sun came in through
the wooden panels
sliced into two thousand pieces
and your skin lit up
like will-o-wisps on steroids.
Your nakedness I wore
like a warm summer sky.
When night came, I stood at your door
you were wearing 711 curtains.
I took them off
so slowly
even the winds stopped to listen.

Fever

By the window, with a hairpin
that kept a waterfall locked in her hair
she's now busy dividing
her thermometer reading
into two unequal parts.
Her face burns
like tail lights
and when I insist on checking myself
she opens the door to a sun
and I warm my hands
around her bonfire breasts.
Finally when I leave, I put the thermometer
in the mouth of the sky.
The stars melt, the fever grows.

POLITICAL POEMS

Dhaka

I

There have been evenings
when my grandmother would weave stories
from the *pashmina* threads of memory.
She would seamlessly arrange all the events
which by then I knew by heart
and she would keep weaving
long narrow, now foreign lanes
which ran like mice throughout the fabric.
She sprinkled a fistful of the Dhaka rains
onto the portions she felt needed
a little more care.
Soft summer evenings would creep into her eyes
taking her to a courtyard
where at first was planted lilies
and then children who couldn't escape the partition.
When I asked her if all this was true
that women were raped, killed and raped again
that men lost their manhood
before they most their lives
she would smile at the Sylhette moon
always an hour and a half here and there
compared to the one in Calcutta,
and say, "Some yarns were sharper than knives."

Kashmir

II

Here I am
writing about my favourite hell
holding a tourist brochure in hand
wondering at the delusion
that proclaims, "Welcome to heaven on Earth."
But in the heaven
that is not on any tourist brochure
tombstones have names.

In Dreams

With hourly news updates
my old city bleeds a little.
The guns go off like
sirens announcing lunch at the warehouse.
A curfew has been imposed on spring
even the flowers look askance
before winking at the bees.
The wind blows through the bullet holes
decorating my city's punctured lungs.
As if in a dream I hear the lanes
call out my name
And as if in a dream
I shut the doors.

Pakistans and Hindustans

The ants on my wall
form a long procession from opposite sides
meeting and greeting each other
sometimes a warm hug, maybe a kind word,
then are on their way.
My grandmother, when alive,
would have hoped people migrated like that
to their Pakistans
to their Hindustans.

Treasures

In the folds of his wallet among other things
he kept winding highways
a train unwilling to arrive
and a pillow no longer receptive
to the nightly rituals of grief.
This was the currency of a land
without identity cards
where a blueprint of the night
lies at bureaucratic desks
and distance between temples and mosques
No one cares to measure.

Mapping Blood

I trace cities on the map
cities which were once my own
Lahore, Delhi, Dhaka.
From the corners of the dog-eared pages
where history has bookmarked the years with blood
I hear men and women wailing
the shadows of who they were
whispering and refusing to walk with them.
I run my fingers all over the atlas
and the tip of my fingers
smell of blood.

Lunch

I spend my lunchtime
watching skin flakes falling off people
as they rush to match the turning of the world.
I take down names, phone numbers
and dreams of a random passer-by.
Once done, I sit at my desk,
writing about plots of land, never too small
for a new grave.
In some distant field
a child finds a grenade pin
in his undercooked rice
and bites into a piece of his home.

Trapped in Subways

Cities, in my grandmother's time
were anchored to the busiest of ghats
so they wouldn't drift away.
They sat like trained dogs
barking at the ghosts
who slipped out of the cemetery
to mingle with the dead
who were yet to die.
Nowadays you can pin
the cities on the clouds
and when it rains
they remain trapped inside subways.

On Writing

Choices

Once in a while
if you ask a poem
it will choose a language and dialect
for itself.
The ones talking of madness in love
not listed or classified
in western medical journals
will slowly tip-toe their way across
your study and pick
Swahili for itself
then stand in front of you
not for your approval
but for a salute of recognition.
Rains that don't descend
on the spurned lovers of the city
you might find
wearing an old Parisian dialect.
Urdu is an automatic favourite with poems
having a graveyard of stories
somewhere in them.
Within such poems you'll find
calendars of the past
preserved in tiny bottles of the monsoon
and courtesan's songs

that sometimes changed
the course of Jhelum, sometimes
the fate of lovers.
You who are reading this
know that some poems write themselves
no matter which language they choose
ending up in hearts
where springs once had
doors slammed upon them.

Twin Cities

I switch between two languages
when writing about you
between Faiz and Shahid
between nights descending on Lahore
and evenings on grocery shops in my neighbourhood.
I slice open with words
dark nights, and paint brush them
over your city and mine
sprinkling Urdu between the stars.
I switch between two selves
when writing about you
one watching the river go by in Banaras
the other burning in Kashmir.

Witness

Agha Shahid Ali visits me
every night I cheat on a poem
or let words slip
like soap on the bathroom floor.
He sits by my bed
mumbling his disapproval of my verse
sneering at my rhyme
jeering at my moon.
On certain nights he asks me
to walk through Lycidas
and write letters to an October autumn.
Walking through subways
I bump into people
whose death certificates
are resting inside classified folders.
Suddenly, without a warning
without advice
Shahid leaves
I am without my poem,
my poem is without a witness.

Masks

When I write in Urdu
the words drag themselves from the right
like children being taken to school
against their will.
The letters set up camp, light a fire
with the remains of their discarded brothers.
In the evening, they sit by a stream
the surface of which is polished mercury.
Halfway through the poem
an unruly couplet wanders off
to a nearby village
and returns smelling of
grandmothers' shawls.
The others, having already reached the end
exchange their masks
and prepare to walk again.

Separation

We are separated
by the air between rooms
and the space inside
the contents of an envelope.
When the city burns
on the wings of the butterfly
somewhere, someone sets
the dogs on men returning home
having sold off
everything that day.
Memory is a foreign tongue
rusting on spiral staircases
that go all the way
to the moon.
At the end, all that remains
is the breath between
a word and it's forgotten meaning.

Vial

My grandmother often told me
when they ran the spectacle
of slicing the country and women
into pieces
she'd keep dreaming of pirates
trapped in an island, so remote
that even the genie in a bottle
had to work overtime to get there.
Letters, written to people
who had fallen out of favour
with maps and compasses
were rescued by boatmen
who, no matter how hard they tried
could not get lost in the ocean.
Her best friend Syeda
was dragged out by men
to be lost without much fanfare.
My grandmother wrote little notes to her
distilled in homeopathic solution
knives, instead of words
so sharp; it would scratch the
Surface of the moon.

The Ledge

It only occurred to me
upon attending the funeral
of a really long poem
that most of the mourners
were street fighters of sorts.
Every evening, words and forms
abandoned, discarded and scratched out
met in an alley
more sinister than politicians
and sparred without gloves or headgear
till one found a place
on a page like this.
The ones who did not make the cut
sat, sharing the tables with patrons
who could furnish no documents
to prove that they love someone else.
When the bars downed the shutters
they gathered on the roof of the night
striking up a conversation
with anyone
going dangerously close
to the ledge.

Empty Pages

The centre of a word
is surrounded by
an abandoned house
around which other discarded words
gather like ghosts of previous occupants.
By the time, I've strung them up
in a meaningful sentence
like rebels at a city square
for public viewing
my notebook has already become
a mass burial ground.
Panic is generally
the colour of empty pages
lying outside the doorstep
basking in the winter sun.
Stretching across the circumference
of that very word
men like me, sip our evening tea
and meditate on a poem like this
all night long.